Mess with a
MESSAGE

Ray 'Misster Ray' Cunningham

Copyright © Ray 'Misster Ray' Cunningham, 2021

Cover image: Flexgraphics

ISBN-13: 978-1-7366962-3-1

*Chocolate*READINGS
ALL THINGS LITERARY

Publisher's Note

Dedication

I could dwell on all the things they said I couldn't do but I'm so blessed for you to read about all the things I've done!

I dedicate this memoir to my deceased grandparents Miles "Bic" Cunningham Sr., Alfred L. Carr, Whilamenia Jackson Cunningham and last living grandparent, Ollie Carr.

I also dedicate this book to my Party of 8 soon to be 9: Tyra, Sydney, Taylor, Alia, Talif, Deuce, Aniyah and Grayson - Uncle Ray loves all of you

Mess with a Message

Foreword

This is the part of the book that people typically don't read. As with most things, we just want to get to the bits that we believe to be most interesting. I don't think I've ever read a foreword in my life, and I am a bibliophile! When Ray asked me to write this for him, I was overcome with excitement. If I'm honest, I worried that I wouldn't be able to do a good job, one that was worthy of the honor. And then I had to think about why I was asked, and I can only guess it's because he knows I have loved him from day one, that I have always believed in him, and that no matter what, I would always be one of his biggest cheerleaders.

Ray has truly lived his life out loud. The Ray you "know" right now, the Mr. Ray who graces your home through television, the one who always has his eyebrows done and comes with the perfect clapback... I didn't know him. I knew the high school Ray Cunningham who was funny and passionate about school spirit. Ray was on my yearbook staff and a member of one of my English classes. That Ray wasn't as sure of himself as a person. He knew he was going to college, and I believe he knew he would be famous someday, but the person, the man...was still trying to find his voice.

This book will take you through Ray's stages, his life. He will stand before you, unclothed, in his greatest form of honesty and humility, to share his humanity. You may shake your head in disbelief, you may laugh, and you may even cry, but in the end, what you should take away from his autobiography, from his "now" life, is that *everything* is possible. Anything you believe you can do is possible. The life you want is awaiting your pursuit and dedication to the dream.

How many of us would be willing to share our first kiss, our first sexual exploit, our insecurities, our depression or our "triggers" with strangers? Who among us has come to a point in our lives where we can honestly say, "This is me, in all my glory and with all my flaws! Take me or leave me," and mean it? What kind of courage would allow someone to bear his soul, open himself up to criticism and degradation and still sleep like a baby at night? Mr. Ray has done it because he has learned to live in his truth, to look people in the eye and say, "What the fuck you thought?"

Read his story. Be inspired or not. Become more empathetic or don't. However, you should search to see yourself in his rise, in his audacity to create the life that he wants. Recognize that he is still in the infancy stages of his greatness. He is seizing every opportunity he has prayed for, and this book, this part of the story, is just the beginning.

Contents

Introduction

I decided long ago
Never to walk in anyone's shadows
If I fail if I succeed
At least I'll live as I believe
No matter what they take from me
They can't take away my dignity

- Whitney Houston

Depending on when you met me, you'll either know me as *Rascal, Little Ray, Gay Ray, Samantha's Little Brother, Myles* not *Miles* or *Misster Ray!* I'm the over-the-top gay friend in everyone's head with no filter, straight outta Virginia. The media over the years has associated the word "messy" with my name, but how am I messy when I'm doing what my job requires in order to keep it? I'm no angel either, I admit I can be playfully messy at times, but I do have something most don't in Hollywood, integrity and a heart. In the book of life, the word *message* has *mess* in it, thus meaning there's a lesson learned in every situation.

Looking back over the last fifteen years of my entertainment career, I've been able to do some cool shit. I've never been pressed to do anything, just blessed to have always been properly positioned with no ulterior intent. If there's one thing I've learned on this journey, it's to be *prepared* and be ready to adapt, improvise and overcome as my father has always told me. I didn't even know who *I* was back then, much less prepared to represent an entire community I wasn't even familiar with at the time. Thankfully, I had some awesome mentors to monitor my crash course in Hollywood but never let me fall flat on my face on their watch.

The coolest part of my journey is it started at the dawn of social media, Facebook launched my junior year of college. From Facebook post, IG photos and Snapchat videos - y'all have seen some of my most memorable moments: me being casted on *College Hill* for BET becoming the first-ever gay to be featured on the network in its than 25 year history, the births of my younger nephews and nieces, enrolling in graduate school, attending President Barack Obama's inaugural ball with Kenya Moore when he was re-elected, sitting between Chris Tucker and Anita Baker at the 2008 *BET Awards* - *oh the commentary from them had me in stitches while Queen Latifah was hosting,* partying with Diddy in Washington DC, hosting WEtv's first ever digital talk show series *100 & Real with Misster Ray,* working with the Biden HBCU and LGBTQ committees during the 2020 election, meeting Vice President

Kamala Harris, my health scares with appendicitis and alopecia.

Most of my bucket list has been checked off but this book is one of the final items I wanted to do and share because majority of the time when I'm on television or you're reading an article about me, it's an **EDIT** of what I fully said and who I am."

I have a strong determination and I'm not afraid of change.

I've been a determined and "push thru" spirit my whole life so with every single set back I've had and situations that should've broken me, didn't. I've learned the hard way, all money and every opportunity isn't necessarily good. I'm a "Hollywood 101" walking billboard for building off of adversity and remaining true to what my initial mission was to do: be a voice for my communities.

Mess with a Message is a memoir from a sippin' Christian who sometimes slips but knows God still me! 15 years later, I'm still here with my original mission with an expanded vision. I've had the unique opportunity to work on camera, behind the camera and in the office - *name someone else who has done the same.* I'm thankful for **EVERY** single opportunity I've had: tv personality, radio personality, acting, producing, casting, entertainment editor, blogger and creative director. My 15 minutes started 15 years ago, and I've learned valuable lessons, so let's say cheers to the next 15!

Enjoy, sip and gag!

Chapter One

Black Boy Joy

"He who is resilient, excellent, capable, & strong. Despite opposition, his strength is not broken. He will remain joyous."

-Unknown

I remember the first time that I heard the phrase *Black Boy Joy*, I instantly connected with it. It did something to my soul. I instantly connected with it because that's exactly how I would describe how my life started out. The energy is amazing, you're smiling from ear to ear; there's not a care in the world – that's Black Boy Joy and that's the environment I was born into, celebrating family and positive accomplishments. Your life is basically put on 'Do Not Disturb' and you get to enjoy every waking moment, peacefully. As a Black man, I rarely get to just sit in and get comfortable in my own skin because of racism and homophobia. With the way life is, there aren't many chances to relax and experience that given the current times we live in.

All day we're getting notifications about life drama, gossip, news, elections, bills, and taxes, and other family drama, friends' drama, depending on where you live, neighbor drama, neighborhood drama, church drama, every aspect of our life comes with some type of drama no matter how much you try to avoid it.

I had a lot of Black boy joy moments in the beginning of my childhood. Early on, my family life was very complex and blended, yet filled with love. I'm a country boy. I grew up in Richmond, Virginia in a *very* nontraditional family. My father and I lived in on the east coast. My mother lived on the west coast. As a kid I didn't understand that I was growing up in a super blended family – I also have a stepmother, stepfather and step siblings. I just always knew that my family was big and that was normal for me. *It didn't seem out of place that I had sisters and brothers with different mothers or that I didn't live with my mom. I just knew that I had a bomb ass life, lived in a big house and every family holiday was a good time.*

My father made sure that we spent a lot of quality time together. Every summer we took a family trip to the beach. My father's job at Amtrak kept him on the road majority of the time but when time permitted, he would take us on his trips up to DC or on his work trips in Florida. My father is one of the least problematic people you'll met – I remember going down to Florida with him for a work conference at

Disney World, they airlines lost our luggage so guess what we did — same in the pool all day. No shower? Order whatever I wanted from room service? My dad never panicked, adapted to the situation and we improvised when most people would be stressed about being out of town with no luggage.

In my opinion, my family is a good time - *the Cunningham's in Virginia and the Carr's in California.* We love the beach. We like a good cocktail. We like watching old Black movies. We are super supportive of each other (most times) and celebrate everything, you hear me! Whether it's a holiday, birthday, or job promotion. Somebody got their ears pierced, you got a new job. We got together, have dinner or something and laugh about old times. So yeah, that was normal for us.

Now, while I loved living with my father, I hated that my parents were divorced. The one thing I didn't mind about not living with my mother is that I'd get to go and visit her in California. Every summer, every birthday, every spring break, every Christmas break, and every fall break, I was able to fly by myself, cross country from Virginia to Los Angeles to be with my mother and her family.

It was like going to another planet. Richmond and L.A. is night and day from each other. It's my kind of different. *I loved that I was able to leave the country and play in the big city for a while.* It felt good being in California and seeing people like myself, gay men but not given the side eye. In L.A., I'm just one of a million gays. I felt like I had a uniform on because compared to LA, Virginia is very conservative and everyone knows my father, one way or another in a good way. When I came to the west coast, I felt like I got to remove the uniform and do what I wanted to do.

Growing up, I just knew about family, not necessarily the dysfunction of it all. I did know about trauma, though. I was existing in the middle of a lot of it.

My family did a *lot* to protect me from whatever it was they felt was the harsh realities of being a Black man, or a Black boy at the time. I come from a very tight knit family – you mess with me, and I had two sisters, Samantha and Angie coming for that ass, ask one of my relatives who tried me over the phone at my *College Hill* premiere when I came out gay, but we'll get into that tea later. If you weren't a Cunningham or family friend, you wasn't around us. It was just that simple. I didn't grow up fighting and hating people.

Despite the fact that I grew up in an overprotective family, I still got molested and still got picked on in school. I was called 'Gay Ray' by my peers for as long as I can remember, and I hated it. *I can laugh now at this while writing but constant taunting is what secretly drove to prove every one wrong one day.* That was such a hard time for me. I don't even know if I understood what gay was but evidently everyone else did. I don't remember any other gay kids growing up in my neighborhood, my church, or my school so if anyone was an unofficial representative for gays, it was me. It's not like I was walking around with a flag and switching. But I definitely had a flick of the wrist and not because I had an iced-out Rolex on. I was definitely feisty and very quick witted. Okay, they knew! Hell, who didn't know?

Yes, it was evident that I was gay. It wasn't a secret, but I didn't discuss it openly either. I didn't think it needed to be discussed because I didn't think I was bothering anybody. The first person I ever came out to was my cousin's wife, Monique Smith and his sister, Tanielle when I was in high school. Not to be fooled, my sister Samantha, she knew too. So again, what was I hiding from? Sissy. Fairy. Punk. Fag. Gay Ass Nigga. You name, I've been called it. So why did I want to address this to welcome more ridicule?

I was born in 1983. Who cared about bullying in the 90s. Our parents were trying to make sure we weren't getting shot over Jordan's. My family would tell me that "...sticks and stones" line but at one point, I was ready to pick those sticks and stones up and beat someone's child ass, but I wasn't a fighter.

When no one stood up for me in class, that told me that I needed to hide who I truly am; hide Mr. Ray. I told myself to just be a mystery. Literally, hide him, keep him secret, don't let anybody see him. I didn't want to embarrass myself or my family. I didn't want my sexuality to hinder me in the long run. I would get into fights and had to defend myself for hanging around girls more than boys, they were jealous that the girls wanted to sit and chat with me instead. One of my childhood bullies from school and the church I grew up in actually ended up being my first sexual partner my junior year of high school. We dated until I went away to college, and he ended up dating a girl I knew from high school.

Ashamed of Success

I have to admit, my Black Boy Joy didn't last too long. You know how life is. Someone just had to do or say *something* that tore me down. And it's not just one thing that stole my joy. Over time, several things that I had gone through stole that feeling away from me. I learned *really* fast that people can snatch your joy away and it can take a lifetime to get it back. *One of the first things to strip me of my joy was feeling ashamed of my father's success.*

Yes, you read that correctly. I was ashamed that my dad was successful.

Now, hear me out. I was already being called 'Gay Ray', so I really wasn't trying to give anyone else another reason to tease me. And I know you're probably thinking, *who would tease you because your father is successful?* Kids, that's who.

Being that my family basically sheltered me, I didn't really understand that people don't need a good reason to dislike you. I think being overprotected by my family kind of kept me blind to a lot of the realities of what the real world was in terms of, everyone isn't going to like you. There are people who don't like you simply because you come from a certain neighborhood or upper middle-class family, they think you got it all, don't know what it means to struggle and everything is handed to you when in reality, we all have daily personal struggles. They just assume that you have no issues and no worries. They believe that you don't work for anything. That's how I felt all through school. I was actually embarrassed when my dad came to school to pick me up from band practice or something student government related. People knew that he was successful because he didn't drive a regular car. My dad drove classic Corvettes and my step mother who was the counselor at my rival high school drove a convertible Mercedes Benz and they kept their cars in immaculate condition. Whenever he'd pick me up, people would stop and stare. I hated that. And I got picked on for it. I got picked on because I wore nice clothes. I remember not wanting to live in our neighborhood and wanted to live down the street in Huntington Village, which was little rough back then but that's where majority of the kids I went to school with lived. I was dumbing myself down so that I could fit in with them so they can feel comfortable about themselves, and I be accepted. See, I started off trying to fit in with the wrong crowd trying to be socially accepted.

It was almost like I couldn't do anything right. I felt like, I'm getting picked on because I'm gay. I'm getting picked on because I'm fat. I'm getting picked on because I'm the only Black kid on the neighborhood swim team. And I'm getting picked on because my parents have money, and we live a certain lifestyle. I was naive, I thought every household was like ours. It was like it didn't matter what I did. It was an issue for somebody. I always said when I get a chance, God, whatever it may be, I'm on the first thing out of here from Richmond. I was tired of it.

Virginia is a Commonwealth state. And it's . You're either Black or white, at the time. Virginia is a Commonwealth state and back when I was growing up – it was white areas you didn't go in or around and vice versa for Black neighborhoods but it was my home, my comfort zone. I don't really recall too much diversity then as it is now in terms of growing up with various nationalities. *Me being gay, Black, and outgoing was not the norm for Virginia in the 90s.* So, all the teasing and bullying I experienced chipped away at the joy that I wanted to hold on to. I felt like I had no experiencing what I was so they didn't understand and couldn't relate. Well, there was *one* person...

Nothing Like A Praying Grandmother

Now, if no one else made sure this Black boy had joy, it was definitely my grandmother, whom I affectionately call Mimi. From the time I can remember, she has always been a loving and supportive force in my life. I've always had this unique bond and unexplainable attachment to her. It's like she's my angel on earth. That's my girl, you hear me! We just recently celebrated her 89th birthday last year.

Okay, wait, let me *properly* introduce her.

So, my grandmother's name is Ollie Ruth Carr from Brokehaven, Mississississippi. and proud graduate of Jackson State University. I feel like she is the reason my alter ego, Rachel, exists. My grandmother is the classiest lady of Alpha Kappa Alpha Sorority, Inc, you will ever meet this side of Jackson, Mississippi. My grandmother is the 'have her pinky finger in the air driving her convertible Benz' kind of classy. As a young kid, my grandmother had me drinking coffee as a common tea, we were eating crab legs, oysters, Thai food and Chinese food. She taught me how to eat with chopsticks. Mimi was all about etiquette and presentation, napkin in the lap, salad fork right before serving knife, spoon, little spoon, salad plate. She was particular about where the plates go, and lord don't let that white kitchen floor not be clean…while she is cooking. I was eating foods that normal kids my age wouldn't eat. I was asking for sushi. I was asking for bacon wrapped scallops, Mexican corn and spicy salsas. I wanted green olives and club soda. I wanted cucumbers and vinegar.

I was always eating different foods when I spent time with her because she wanted me to expand my palate. She'd say, "In Virginia they don't eat nothing but every part of the pig so when you're here, you're going to try everything so you can acquire your own taste." No shade to the hog lovers, I love my bacon and chitlins too!

My grandmother sent me to the finest of dining all over Los Angeles from Compton to Watts, Long Beach, Santa

Monica, Venice, Beverly Hills, Pasadena, you name it. There wasn't an area my grandmother did not take me because she said she wanted me to be well versed and well-educated in different types of food, cultures and be able to adapt to any room I walk into.

Now, I'm going to be transparent with you and don't you laugh at me. Outside of the Asian family that grew up in our neighborhood, it wasn't too much diversity until I went to California.

Growing up in Virginia, you either see Black people or white people. Now mind you, there's Chinese food in Richmond. There's Taco Bells and Mexican restaurants all over Virginia, but I had never met anyone from those ethnic backgrounds. So, coming to L.A. I just felt like I was always going to a new world, like I was learning new stuff and I *loved* it! The first time I had Hot Cheetos was when one of my little Hispanic homeboys in L.A. gave me some at summer camp. I was hooked! They didn't have Hot Cheetos at that time in Virginia, so I would have my grandmother mail me boxes of them.

Everything that I wanted, my grandmother made sure that I had it. She was always there for me. Like, if my dad put me on punishment in Virginia and I couldn't watch the Soul Train awards, who would record it for me in LA and had it for me when I got there for the summer? My Mimi. I wanted some new Jordan's, but my parents wouldn't get any. Well, who would get them for me? My Mimi. Being the first-born grandchild for her, I got a pass on a lot of things, but my Mimi didn't tolerate back talk.

Hindsight, *I have to admit that my grandmother was always my enabler, but it was an enabler in a good way because she knew that I was a good kid.* Okay, let's call her an advocate. Yes, she was an advocate for me. I didn't have bad grades in school, that was never an issue. I believe she realized that I was, *ahem,* different. My parents probably knew too but chose to ignore it. I think my Mimi was aware of this and just wanted me to be comfortable. That might have turned into spoiling me a little bit, but I wasn't a totally bad kid – I was diagnosed as having ADHD and took Ritalin for it. Mimi told my mom I didn't need to start elementary school at the time I did because I was either going to make the teacher drink or I was going to get kicked out of the school for my behavior. She was right, after I finished pre-school my teacher Ms. Wong quit teaching and I ended up getting kicked out after first grade for my disruptive behavior. Again, I was undiagnosed at the time. Once I was on the medication, I was a different person and now even as an adult, I take Adderall to help myself stay focused. You never outgrow having ADHD.

Along with my grandma being a certified diva, she's a highly educated woman. My grandparents relocated from Mississippi to California where she began working for the L.A. Unified School District. She retired as a Guidance Counselor from Compton High school and during her time there, she says she recalls Dr. Dre, Easy E, Ice Cube and later Tyrese and his brother being her students. My Mimi was in these streets, she always had to best studio copies of the bootleg DVDs.

My Mimi has always been my soft spot. She's always been my biggest cheerleader, my biggest supporter. She probably knew I was gay before I said I was gay. But she allowed me to say it on my own terms, when I was ready; she didn't want to take that moment away from me and I'll always adore her for that.

So yes!

I loved being around my grandmother as a young boy because I was able to be myself. The moments when situations stole my joy, she would give me the best advice followed by a story of her own trial and errors. The relationship that I had with my grandmother as a young boy truly shaped who I am as a man. It helped to build my confidence. It showed me that it was okay to be different. That I didn't have to put myself in a box or stay in the box that others tried to fit me in. While I will always appreciate my grandmother for being the reason, I held on to the little joy that I had left, something

tragic would happen to this little Black boy
that would turn my joy into a deep sorrow...

Chapter 2

Boy Interrupted

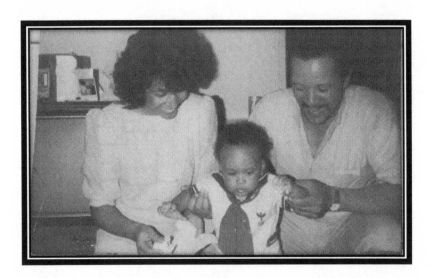

"Don't be embarrassed of your situation. Half of these people are covering up the same situations with filters and smiles. Make a plan, cut off distractions, stay focused and execute consistently. You'll make it. I promise."

-Unknown

Like most Black kids, I grew up in the era where you didn't question adults, and you didn't tell your parents business to nobody. If you're like me, at some point during your childhood you heard the phrase: 'What goes on in this house stays in this house' more times than you care to remember. I took that toxic phrase to heart. While this may have been a rule for many Black households, now that I'm grown, I don't agree with that mess. Because I didn't question adults and was afraid to tell somebody when traumatic things happened to me, the joy that I did have as a young boy was **SEVERELY** interrupted. And you know what? I didn't tell anybody immediately because no one asked, so, I didn't tell.

Life for me was pretty positive and happy up to the day my **LIFE WAS FOREVER CHANGED**. I was repeatedly sexually abused by a babysitter's son, and I didn't tell anyone for a very long time. I knew it was wrong because I didn't see it happening with any of the other kids that were around me. I never heard it mentioned when hanging with other boys at school.

Although I had no one to compare stories with, in the back of my mind, I knew something wasn't right.

When I would spend time at my babysitter's house with her children, we would watch the Black romantic comedies. We'd always pretend to cover our eyes during the inappropriate parts. I remember the adults would send us upstairs to go to sleep, but actually, it would be time for me to put on a show. I've been technically an actor since I was 7. And I'm saying this in a joking way because it's kind of hard to say this without feeling some type of way. My babysitter's son used to make me his leading actress and role play. I was one of the women who "cleaned the royal penis" like in *Coming to America*. We would be upstairs in his room because that's where I would sleep, and he would make me role play with him. The things that we were seeing on TV, we were acting it out in person. His mother would be in her room with no clue that her son was violating me and making me his bitch. Thinking back on it, his room felt like a jail cell, and I was his sexual prisoner.

Before you think to yourself, "Why didn't you say anything?" Well, I don't know. I knew something was different about it. I can't tell you that I liked it. But I knew that I was comfortable with it. And as I got older, and I started to identify those feelings and begin to understand that I'm gay but that did not make the situation right.

But we'll talk more about that in a later chapter.

After my innocence was stripped from me, life changed for me. At the time, I was living with my mother, and I remember her response being "how is this my fault?" but after I told my stepmother they made sure that I stayed far away from my abuser, which meant that I didn't get to live with my mother anymore, and that was difficult.

It was hard to grasp my mind around the fact that I'm the reason the courts took me from my mother because I exposed an ugly truth that mentally fucked me up. Oh, because honey it was a whole thing! I had to speak to a judge, go to therapy, all of the above. I felt bad because everyone was blaming my mother not my abuser.

To be very clear on the record with everybody. Here's the message in this mess: I've always liked boys. I knew I liked boys as a kid. I remember kissing a boy in daycare. First boy I ever kissed was a white boy. I remember kissing him in the bathroom and the teacher catching us and she saying, "cut that sissy shit out". Now, I'm not saying that I was only kid acting out what they saw on television, but difference was, I was forced. I'm saying I acted out what I felt, and I was attracted to boys, and he took advantage of me being a young questioning gay kid.

What society has to understand is that just because a boy is gay doesn't mean he wants someone to take advantage of him or introduce him to sexual acts before his mind and body can handle it. Whether I was gay as a kid or not, I was not ready to be intimate in anyway with anyone and that changed my life forever.

Where Was Mama?

Most people always wonder where the primary parent was when their child was being violated. Well, I can't speak for everyone else's mother, but mine was working a lot. My mother was just you know, being the best single mom that she knew to be with the support of my father. She and my dad divorced so she had to do what she had to do. When my parents divorced, my mom did not relocate to Los Angeles right away. She stayed in Virginia for a while. Maybe she wanted my father to be in my life, maybe she really liked it, not sure why she stayed. Well, it's not like she wasn't holding it down. She was a supervisor at Philip Morris, made good money and lived over in the south side of Richmond. After a while, she attempted to date, and I wasn't really feeling that. I remember my mom had boyfriends – they were all trash. There's one boyfriend in particular who would beat on me when she would be at work. I never told my mom, but I remember telling my dad and anyone that would listen. And you know what? They charged it all to my imagination.

Again, I was undiagnosed at the time, and no one knew why I was so hyper.

Adults not believing me contributed to me putting my feelings in my back pocket. If they think I'm playing about being verbally and physically abused, what would they think if I told them about the sexual abuse?

At the end of the day, I don't blame my mother for what happened to me. It's not her fault that a space she thought was safe was held with a monster. It's also not my fault, whether I like men or not – violating me was disgusting. It's just something that happened, and I choose to extend grace to my mother, forgive and move forward.

How 'bout *that* for some tea!

And Then There Was Therapy

So, after moving in with my dad and stepmom, they felt the need to get Little Ray some help, so they put me in therapy. Originally the reason for me going to therapy was because I had been molested,

40

that quickly included my behavior as well because I start showing my ass, with good reason. Now, let me explain just how quickly my life changed. On Sunday I was with the babysitter, Monday I was dropped off at daycare by my mother and picked up and living with my father by Tuesday. So, in three days, my world shifted for good. No young child can handle that much change in such a short amount of time. Hell, I'm an adult and I still get dizzy thinking about it.

Now, I'm a child when all of this is happening, so I can't quite grasp that something is wrong at the time, but I know something is up. After my dad picked me up, not only did he get full custody of me, but I didn't get to see my mom again until middle school. My grandmother told me after my mother lost custody of me, she had a mental breakdown and didn't cope well with the judge's decision. I was in the third grade when I moved with my dad. I was not allowed to have conversations with her on the phone that were not supervised. I thought I was in juvie!

When I came to live with my dad, they did everything in their power, within reason, to wipe that first part of my life away. There was no more spending the night at people's houses, that wasn't an immediate relative. They censored the TV I was watching. I had a schedule, my stepmother created to keep me, um, focused. She scheduled everything, you hear me. When I came home from school, I was expected to immediately sit at the table, start my homework, eat my dinner, finish up my homework afterwards, bathe by 8 o'clock and TV off by nine o'clock.

Yep, that was my life for years. Like, I literally I felt like I was a Stepford wife.

This was the other reason I was in therapy. I was going crazy. So much so that I ended up getting prescribed to take Ritalin finally after I was successfully diagnosed. I hated taking that medicine. Whenever I would take it, I felt like I was watching myself in third person. That's how I felt for years! And I couldn't put that into words, so you know what I did? I started acting a damn fool. Between feeling bad about being forced to live with my dad and being teased for my mannerisms, life just wasn't fun for me. I remember telling my dad about being teased. I say to him, "They're calling me fat. They're calling me a sissy."

I felt my dad didn't take me seriously and I begin to resent him. Part of his not being in tuned with me was because he was on the road for work providing for us siblings.

I resented living at my new home not because I was ungrateful, but I missed my mama. Looking back, I think it was the best decision. To keep it all the way real, had my father not gotten custody of me and put the things he put in place to help me restructure my life, I would not be where I am right now. So thank you, dad and Phyllis for that.

But listen, I don't know why they thought therapy would work. I don't remember nothing about that therapy. I just wanted it all to be over, so I told them what they wanted to hear. I'm not going to lie to you. I didn't put in any effort because I was resentful. I was mad, not at my dad for making me go, but at myself for telling our secret. I got my mom in trouble.

When my mom left and went to California, I felt like she took my happy with her. All I knew in my life was my mom, whether how well we got along or how well we did not get along. How are we you know, it didn't matter. That was my mom. That's who I lived with. That's who I woke up to. That's who I was cooking with. That's who I was playing with. That's who was disciplining me; that's who was rewarding me. She was there for me and then, she wasn't.

For years I blamed myself for my mother's unhappiness with losing custody of me. I took on my mother's disappointment of her losing custody of me and me not living with her. But now, I release that burden.

The Mess In This Message: Deliver Me

The one thing I learned from experiencing my joy being interrupted is that the Black community has to do better with protecting our children and exposing predators. We are taught certain values and ways to deal with things in a way that doesn't negatively impact the family and not fair to the person experiencing the trauma. I internalized so much hurt, pain, and trauma for the sake of protecting the image of my family. I was silenced and taught that keeping my mouth closed made me conservative and made thing appear right. When in actuality, it deepened my wounds and contributed to the hole in my soul. Silencing my truth taught me to dumb down how I felt and who I was so that I could fit the mold or the projected stereotype that's expected of me.

I'm grateful for the two dynamic families that I was born into. However, I've decided to define my life on my terms now.

Reclaiming My Joy

Baby, when I heard aunty Maxine Waters says she's reclaiming her time, I felt that! That's what I had to do over the years for my inner peace, reclaim that thang! I had to take my joy back. Donald Lawrence's song *Deliver Me* with LeAndria Knight ministered to me in such a way that I had to pull over, cry and had to release my hurt —

"He leads me beside still waters
He restoreth my soul
When you become a believer
Your spirit is made right
And sometimes, the soul doesn't get to notice
It has a hole in it
Due to things that's happened in the past
Hurt, abuse, molestation
But we wanna speak to you today and tell you
That God wants to heal the hole in your soul
Some people's actions are not because their spirit
is wrong
But it's because the past has left a hole in their
soul
May this wisdom help you get over your past
And remind you that God wants to heal the hole
in your soul"

That song had me on the side of the 405 Freeway in Los Angeles crying my eyes out and on repeat. I've never heard a song that ministered to me like that. It's so easy to place our pain into other people's hands. I've learned they can hold or even cause it, but they can never make you carry that pain. It's up to you to release it. And that's what I've been doing. Releasing my pain and reclaiming my Black boy joy because I deserve it.

Chapter 3

Virginia Made, BET Paid!

"Life is not being rich, being popular, being highly educated or being perfect. It is about being real, being humble, and being kind."

-Unknown

My Virginia State University experience is one that I will *never* forget. It literally changed my life. I had no clue that me going to an HBCU would lead to me being a part of the cast on America's first ever reality series, *College Hill* on BET.

Now, that was not my first choice. I really wanted to go to Morris Brown. That was like the big popular school at the time and let's keep it real, the mecca for gays and I wanted to be where the action was. *Drumline* was really popular at the time and so I wanted to go to Morris Brown. My grandmother wanted me to go to Jackson State like she did. That was out as far as my father was concerned. Of course, my grandfather wanted me to go to Tugaloo College where he graduated from in Mississippi. That was definitely out as far as my father was concerned. I let my family know I had my heart set on Morris Brown, but they were having financial issues, and my aunt Rita told my dad I shouldn't apply because she had heard that the school would be closing, and eventually they did.

Now I'm back to square one. Where am I going to college? After going back and forth with my dad about what school he was willing to pay for, we decided on Virginia State because to keep it real, I didn't have out of state grades. Virginia State was up the highway from where I grew up and many of my elders had also graduated from VSU, including my step mother. VSU was familiar territory for me, as a family we regularly tailgated at the Gold Bowl and Freedom Classic against Virginia Union in Richmond, VA. Thankfully so, I was accepted to VSU. Again, our steps are ordered we just have to follow and have faith of what God has for us down the road.

The Chosen One

I will never forget the moment I was selected to be on *College Hill*. It was definitely one of the best moments of my life. Now, me getting on the show wasn't something that I was seeking, it just kinda presented itself to me and I wanted it.

Okay, here's the tea: I didn't audition the way everyone else did. The show creator, Tracey Edmonds chose me because my name kept coming up in casting from the other students auditing.

Okay, so tea, Tracy Edmonds came to my band practice while we were rehearsing for the homecoming halftime show. She came up to me and said, "I'm Tracy Edmonds." I was like, "Girl, I know who you are, I read my grandma's JET magazines!"

My grandmother would send me Jet magazines to read when I went back home to Virginia. So, I knew who she was from the magazine. She said, "I'm the owner of Edmonds Entertainment. We are working with BET. We are shooting the third season of *College Hill* here at Virginia State." I knew the show she was talking about. I listened as she continued speaking. She mentioned that the show would have totally different look than what I've seen before on BET. She said, "We're filming here, and I actually want to invite you to an interview." I could NOT believe this! Tracey Edmonds wanted to interview little ole me.

Leading up to the day I was chosen was so crazy! Rumors were flying all over campus about who's going to be on the cast. In my mind, I just know I'm gonna be on this cast. Who is better than me to represent this university, hell I was the mascot! It has to be me. An announcement was made that the cast will be revealed during homecoming week, so I was nervous and excited at the same time. Monday went by, nobody heard nothing.

Tuesday went by nobody heard anything.

Wednesday went by nobody heard anything.

Thursday went by... still nothing.

Okay, now what's *really* good? They got us all excited and anxious for nothing! Does it really take this long to choose who can be on a show and its homecoming week, so I was already busy with my obligations as the Trojan mascot? It was starting to get real crazy at VSU. The longer they delayed the announcement, people started to get antsy. It turned into pandemonium on campus. The tensions were high about who was going to be casted. And a lot of us that auditioned were senior Mass Communication majors and had classes together.

Finally, Friday had arrived when they announced who would be a part of the cast of *College Hill* season three. The camera crew walked in, and we all knew what was up. The energy in the class shifted. You can feel how nervous we were. We're all anxious, hoping it's one of our name being called and it's my last class of the day. The president of the University is there so this is it; it's happening. She picks up this piece of paper, reads it and says, "Do you have a Ray in this class?" You can see my class mates reaction on the first episode of the show – everyone was screaming and cheering for me while the other 4 people who had auditioned with me, was just sitting there looking defeated. First lesson in entertainment: everyone can't get the gig.

Listen! I was so excited I couldn't even speak. I was happy. I was emotional. It was such an overwhelming experience. Everybody was yelling and cheering for me. The students ran out on the yard and was shouting and supporting me, it was just so surreal. I couldn't believe it. I got selected! It was the best moment of my life, and I immediately knew that my life was gonna change in that moment. And I was ecstatic about that!

Look, I was a hot damn mess at that time in my life. I had no direction. I had no idea who Ray was. I was just little Ray with a bunch of secrets and somewhat of a closeted gay, to my family. I wasn't sure but I was open to allowing this show to take me on a journey – and it damn sure did.

Call Me Uno Because I Did It First

Now, anyone who has eyes could see that I was gay. However, I never said it out loud at the time except in private discussions with my college girlfriends – Fatimah, Rashawnda, Adrienne, Kayla, Chenee, Jessica, Ashley and Nalini. So being the first gay talent on BET was a heavy crown on my head. Oh, there is definitely shade in this message.

Although I knew I was gay at the time of being on *College Hill*, I wasn't quite ready to say it to the world, or my father - but I did. Through a series of interviews I told my truth. It was pieced together when the show was edited and that's how my opening package was put together. I didn't get a chance to discuss this with my family, so I was terrified. The content was captured and there was no turning back.

Are you sipping this tea yet?

Okay so, I was scared! Every day I was googling BET *College Hill*, Virginia State University to see if anything comes up about me telling my business. And one day, something popped up. I felt like my soul left my left my body. Time was still and I was numb as I read the headline. The article said that show was returning with a cast member that has an alternative lifestyle. My heart dropped. I knew they were talking about me because Rodney, Will and Arlando weren't gay. Then I saw the description. It said, "Ray, school mascot, has an alternative lifestyle." BET would never say gay, but I knew what that meant – and so did my family.

I begged production not to air that. I did *not* want my dad to see that. I was emailing everybody you hear me! I was having anxiety attack. I just knew that my world was going to stop once that press release was out. Mind you, this all went down in December. They sent me a DVD a couple weeks prior with the soundbite that made me cringe. Still, they said that they were going to handle the situation with care, and they didn't. I couldn't be mad and learned yet another tv lesson: what you don't say, they can't air.

Before you ask me why I didn't sue, or whatever, remember we are the first ever African American reality television series. So, our contract compared then to now is night and day. I'm pretty sure the terms are completely different now. But basically, there was nothing I could do because they owned me, my likeness and image a year after the date of the final episode airing. I learned firsthand that production can exaggerate what they want to, they can air what they want to. They basically had power to do whatever they wanted to do. Here I am, the "bitch" yet again in another situation.

I did express to them that this was a very touchy subject. I remember begging and begging and begging. I did not want my dad to find out this way and I wasn't really ready to face that truth. I was scared, pissed off, hurt, and so confused! What was I supposed to do?

I eventually called my cousin Tiffani, and I cried to her. I told her all about how this soundbite of one of my interviews mentioned that *"I'm gay, my mother knows but my father doesn't"*. I hadn't told my father yet, and I was scared. She told me to tell my father so he can process it all before the world sees it. She said, "Don't let this air and your daddy see it on TV."

I should have taken her advice, but I just could not bring myself to tell my dad. I couldn't find the words, nothing would come out of my mouth when I tried to speak about it. I wasn't even trying to promote *College Hill* anymore. He'd asked when the premier is airing and I'd be like, *"College Hill,* premier? I don't know when it is." Lying my ass *off,* you hear me! I was so mad at myself I didn't know what to do. I was not excited about the premiere at all. It wasn't fun anymore. It was like a countdown to coming out to my dad and family… and the world.

To be honest, it's hard to deny that I'm gay. So, I guess this was God's way of telling me to stop pretending. I couldn't hide it anymore if I wanted to anyway. It was on all the college or press releases that I was a school mascot who had an alternative lifestyle.

Fast forward past the family fall out I got to tell my story and become the first *openly* gay talent that BET had on air, but I ain't the first gay talent they had. With the popularity of the show, some of the university staff didn't agree with the content – specifically one of my professors who just happened to be the dean of my department at the time. Some other professors wouldn't let us in class and refused work, if we were late because production took us to and from campus, filming everything. To my knowledge, production had free reign to film us 24/7 literally on and off of campus. So aside from trying to dodge production so they wouldn't catch me doing something else "gay" on camera, I was dealing with the university backlash on campus from some faculty members. One of my professors actually failed me unfairly exaggerating his reasonings for my non-passing grade so two days before graduation with the show still airing, I found out I didn't meet the academic requirements to graduate that weekend and once again after my father and I were in a better place, I let him down I felt. I had to take a three-week course in summer school and had to fly back from Los Angeles in December to participate in winter commencement.

Now sip on *that* tea!

Getting the BET Bag... Kinda

So, remember I said that I knew my life was going to change? Well, an opportunity arose for me to work closely with BET as an intern, and I took it. While I was interning, *College Hill* was still airing but that didn't stop my hustle. I was working with high profile talent, working events - the BET awards, the Hip Hop Awards, the Celebration of gospel, Rip the Runway and Spring Bling. You name it, I'm working with different talent, doing activation setup, the press credentials, prep, all that stuff – and I loved every second it and was putting my degree in Public Relations to good use.

Although I was behind the scenes more, I was still getting my little fifteen minutes of fame because I was one of the fan favorites for my season. I was looking forward to doing more appearances now that I'm working at BET. I mean, I got the hook up so why not. Now, keep in mind, we're still in the era when being gay is just tolerated, not celebrated. And here I am "Gay Ray from BET" in full effect, honey! There's no mistaking my sexuality when you see me, and this make *some* men uncomfortable, including the big wigs at BET.

You have more tea? Let's keep sippin'.

So, at the time, I was interning in the development department. I knew that they were developing some new shows and were discussing what type of people they wanted to cast. One particular show was called *Black Carpet*, and they wanted a celebrity co-host. They wanted someone who was over-the-top to give correspondence in L.A. and at events. **HELLO THAT'S ME!** When I overheard that I was like *yaaaas!* That's right up my alley. In my intern role, I would go to these events on behalf of BET, promoting talent, as well as my participation on *College Hill*. So, in my mind, since that's what I was already doing, this would be the perfect position for me to transition to another show. I'm going to pitch myself.

Now, I can understand that every opportunity isn't for me. Maybe I'm not experienced enough. Maybe I don't have the credentials. Being told that I wasn't qualified because America was not interested in seeing a Black gay man on TV giving commentary because that's a woman's job was devastating. And a smack in the face.

That's what was said to me by a since fired executive when I asked to audition. He said no, explained why he said no, and then gave the job to Toccara Jones from *America's Next Top Model*. Talk about the shade, honey! When I say I was pissed, oh baby, I was *pissed*. I was mad about that for the longest time. And what upset me the most is that Black gay men are the foundation of Hollywood – who do you think these "over the top" ladies get their lingo and mannerisms from, **US**!

Anyway.

I decided that I wouldn't let another human being tell me what they are or not ready for. That's when I decided to be me unapologetically. Gay and all, I am not going **ANYWHERE**. I'm not going to dumb down who I am anymore and I'm going after every opportunity I want to pursue.

As devastated and disappointed that I was, I understood. I knew that I was ahead of my time because there were only **ONE** other Black gay man on TV at the time – Karamo Brown on MTV's *The Real World*.

While I understand the time we were in, it's still not fair. I felt like I had gotten the short end of the stick in terms of and opportunities and turned down several because they only wanted me for "gay antics" and was on concerned about gossip and mess, not who I actually was as a person. Now, it's completely different. There's a lane for Black gay men in the entertainment industry now but more so still for antics and the accessory to these women who imitate us but get paid top dollar.

I took the kicks, the bruises, the rejection and not so courteous remarks online so that a lot of these new people can walk, run and wear their "outfits" unapologetically on camera. A lot of us that started around the same time that were the first of our eras and of our networks – Miss Jay was on CW, Karamo was on MTV, Derek J was Bravo, I believe *RuPaul's Drag Race* was just starting and I was on BET. We had to be ourselves and do what we're doing at the beginning of our careers unapologetically, proudly and **STILL WORKING FIFTEEN YEARS LATER!** That's why these other men can come on TV and be as extravagant and fabulous as they are – **BECAUSE OF US**. I proudly wear my OG crown because before me it was **NONE**. When I started, there was no space for me, now I am the space these networks want to be integrated with.

BET Taught Me

Working at BET taught me the power of networking. I learned that it's all about who you know and relationships. It doesn't matter if you're the plus one, the plus of a plus or working the event – market yourself, sell them your talents and personality! **PERSONALIY GOES FURTHER THAN LOOKS AT THE END OF THE DAY!** The key is to network, look your best and do your research. Prepare yourself just so you don't get caught slipping for knowing or having not having accurate information about someone because Hollywood is small, and you don't want to be labeled negatively. People are always looking for a reason to write someone off in Hollywood to eliminate the competition.

Like if you know you're going to a Revolt event, there's a possibility that Diddy just may be there or if he's not there, someone from his camp will be there. You have to imagine the ten degrees of separation. Anything is possible. I was going to these events, taking pictures with everybody. I'm taking shots with everybody. I'm having a good time with everybody. I was excited to be there. I was living in the moment.

When I was working at BET, it was like attending a family reunion with your favorite cousins every day. Of course we've all seen the *Boondocks* episode, but I can honestly confirm that's not how meetings go and no one has an agenda to make Black people look bad. Yes it's a relaxed dress code but it wasn't a club either. Only the strong survived working at BET, it was a fast-paced environment where only the strong survived. I was fortunate to learn so much while working with the Corporate Communications department under some amazing ladies whom I will always have a special place in my heart for. I've made some lifelong friends that worked at BET —

Carma, Mimi, Robyn, Tosha, Zabrina, Voncella and Leslie. BET will forever be my first love in entertainment because they introduced me to world and allowed me to live out some of my wildest dreams. BET is home to so many greats in our community and I'm blessed to be amongst there names of the people who've gone on to do great things.

Chapter 4
Out of the Closet!

"Everybody's journey is individual. If you fall in love with a boy, you fall in love with a boy. The fact that many Americans consider it a disease says more about them than it does about homosexuality."

– James Baldwin

Saying that Ray is gay should be almost as normal as saying the sky is blue. Anyone looking at me as a boy could tell that I did not have any interest in girls other than being their friend. **KEEP THAT OVER THERE HUNNY AND BRING ME THE MEAT!** It definitely wasn't a secret. It shouldn't have been a surprise in my personal opinion. I mean, you can look back at old VHS tapes my father has and see me with my hand on my hip, neck rolling, and fingers popping. The only thing I didn't have was a ponytail and some lip gloss, Ray Jr. wasn't having that under his roof!

What you see now is what I've always been. I've always been sassy, quick-witted; snapping one-liners, and cracking funny jokes. I've always been the over-the-top, good time, life of the party friend. I think because I've always been overly active, my family chose to ignore my sexuality and just accept my colorful personality, which is fine by me because does it really matter? My sexuality didn't stop my family from loving me so just like they swept it under the rug, and so did I. When I did finally come out, indirectly of course, I don't think anyone was shocked, but more so let down.

I could imagine my parents thinking how disappointed I made them feel. I'm my mother's first and only child; my dad's first and only son, I'm from a very traditional family – and I have the audacity to be gay. My mom's reaction was: *Well, I already knew, I don't know how your dumb ass dad couldn't see that.*

Now, while it may have never been a conversation with my family, or with myself for that matter, my sexuality was something that was a part of who I am as a person. I didn't have to come out of a closet because I wasn't in one. Since a young boy, I was attracted to other boys so that was my version of coming out! But I will say this, I ignored the fact that I liked boys for a long time. I knew my dad would be upset, so I tried my best to pretend I wasn't gay. I was out here liking girls that liked girls, but for picture purposes it worked. It was hard because my dad was making me play a bunch of sports which I didn't mind – the boys on the swim team wore speedos and the boys on the basketball had basketball shorts for practice – ladies and gays, you know what I'm referring to. I was having to get dressed and undressed in front of a bunch of boys and I was here for it! However, I didn't want to have those thoughts because I didn't want anyone to know much less get beat up for staring. If I entertained some of the thoughts I had, I'd be walking around that locker room with a boner, and that wouldn't have been cool at all. So, for years, I just ignored my feelings and suppressed my thoughts.

And then one day I stopped ignoring those feelings and suppressing my thoughts.

Okay, so tea!

I had my first consensual sexual encounter in high school with one of my childhood bully's.

You sippin'?

So yep, one of my bully's took my virginity. Now that may sound weird but hear me out. He wasn't a complete stranger. He was someone that I grew up with, so I felt comfortable with him. Well, after I was sure that he wasn't setting me up. I ain't no fool.

You're probably thinking, *how in the hell did I link up with my bully.* You remember the party line back in the day?! Well, that was my way of finally starting to get comfortable talking about my sexuality. I had heard that they had a line specifically for gay men, so I needed to see what that was about. To my surprise, I hop on and hear a very familiar voice. He has a distinct ring to his voice, so I knew who it was right away. I've heard this voice all my life – and I couldn't believe it.

The very person who beat me up for switching and 'acting gay' is on the party line for gay men.

Mmmkay, sir.

Initially, I didn't say anything to him because I still wasn't sure if it was him or not. Apparently he recognized my voice too because eventually he hit me up – and it was him. After getting past the initial shock of the mystery voice, I sat on that chat line listening to this man tell me that he's always loved me. He's always liked me. And he's always wanted to tell me, but you know, it's not cool to be gay.

I wish I could tell ya'll who I'm talking about because you wouldn't even believe me. He was the most homophobic person you could think of. He was an avid church goer, very much so masculine – and he wanted to fuck me.

Ha!

So, we actually linked up... Don't judge me! But yes, we did. I had a sneaky link before it was a thing! Since I had a car, we'd sneak and link up. I remember the first time we met up. I didn't just jump his bones right away, though. I had to make sure he wasn't trying to play me. I went by his place. And we talked. Plus, I wanted to make sure that I was really into him. And it was just like this moment, like, *wow*. I couldn't believe this was happening. We clicked, we were vibing. We were feeling each other, and we actually did it.

And we *kept* doing it.

We ended up doing it all through my sophomore, junior and senior year in high school. Sneaking around, driving to different places. We eventually stopped talking because I went off to college. I don't know where he is right now, but all I know is that one of my childhood bully's ended up becoming my first boyfriend.

Go ahead and pour another cup of that tea!

Being A Gay Black Man in Hollywood

I've learned not to be ashamed of being a Black, gay man early on. I also learned that society doesn't view me as equal, and that makes me feel a ways. One thing I want people to know is that Black gay men are not accessories. We are people. Stop putting us in the role of your sidekick, wing man, best friend, the over-the-top flamboyant embellishment. People do it in real life and in entertainment and it sucks! We're never just the lead. We're always looked at as an agenda, a topic, or an accessory, and I'm tired of that. I hate that. There are so many different types of gay. And I know for me, I've struggled with that in my career because once Hollywood gets locked into an image of what a certain gay looks like, they want everyone to look like that. Sorry I'm not wearing a wig for a check.

At one point in time, they wanted the overly masculine but surprised he's gay looking guy. Then it went to the metrosexual gay guy. Then it went to the overly masculine gay guy. Then it was the overly flamboyant gay guy. They want everyone to look and act the same. And do this and do that. Or everything is a gay joke. Or something's overly sexualized. And they get into these fads of what we are. And if you don't fit that fad, then it's almost like you're not relevant to that moment.

I've maintained the same personality and Hollywood hasn't changed me. I refuse to change who I am, just so that I can stay a part of the conversation. Some people are masculine on one show, they come back on the next gig, and they're a little bit more conservative. The next year, they're overly flamboyant, and overly gay. And then the next one, they're like, totally a different person. I don't believe in changing my game to fit the gig — *take me as I am or have nothing at all.*

In television, you have three types of gays: feminine, masculine, and dramatic butch queen – *that's me!* TV producers typically tend to cast these types of gays and put us against each other. And I don't like it. Either have this extremely uptight, upscale gay, or you have this extremely gutter rat gay. There's never one in between. And, though it makes good TV, I feel like it divides us as a community because there's a wide spectrum of gay. There's levels to this.

If I had to give some advice, I'd tell young, Black gay men the most important thing we have individually is our voices. Nobody can tell our story the way we can tell our own stories. No one can tell my story for me the way I'm telling my story right now.

Take Me As I Am

At this point if you don't know I'm gay, then girl, I don't know where you've been! My name is Misster Ray. I have two S's in my name for a reason. Use the context clues. Once my father accepted my coming out on television, he told me "Your last name is still

CUNNINGHAM and your personal preference doesn't define who you are, it's a part of your life but it's not your life. Let your name speak for you when you walk into a room, you don't have to announce you're gay to get attention." I took what my father said to heart and decided to own the taunting of being called **GAY RAY** to **MISSTER RAY**. The two S's represents my **PRIDE**, but it's still spelled **MISTER** and that's adhortative in itself to call me **MISTER**.

I'm 100% confident in my skin. You can't tell me just anything and I accept it. You can't piss in my face and tell me its lemonade. I know who I am. I know what I'm about. I know what I want to be. I know who I can be. And I'm doing everything I've learned to just live in the moment.

I'm a living testimony of how God's timing works and to not question things. I try not to ever go according to my own plan. When it happens, it happens. Your life is already written. You just have to align yourself so that you can live it. **RIGHT** and walk in your **LIFE**.

Oh my God... I sound like my dad!

Chapter 5

The Level Up

You know, be able to do something great in your life, you're gonna have to realize your failures. You're gonna have to embrace them and figure out how to overcome it.

– Dave Chappelle

I always knew that I was destined to do great things. I just always had this ball of creativity brewing in me, of course, I just didn't know how to channel that creativity. That is, until I met Pam. Back in 2008, Pam became my business partner and together, we launched my company, Social Status. I met her through one of my girlfriends, Saaphyri. Ironically, she was working as an executive over at Fox Reality Network, but we never crossed paths until I saw her over on 54th and Crenshaw getting her edges laid. Saaphyri was actually on *Flavor of Love* at the time, but she still kept working in her salon. Pam was one of her clients. So, when I came in there one day just to visit and catch up with her, she introduced me to Pam and just like that, we became friends.

Our friendship turned into a business partnership once we realized that we worked well together. We worked on a couple of projects, and Pam thought it would be dope to start a PR company and I was here for it. We started out doing free consultations, and eventually we started charging. We've worked with some of everybody! From *America's Best Dance Crew* to the women that were on *Flavor of Love*, we've worked with New York, Omarosa, Jamie Foxx, and NBA legend, Dominic Wilkinson, just to namedrop a lil' bit. Our most fun event was Lisa Raye's 50th birthday party. There would be no Lisa Raye party without our first client, though: Claudia Jordan.

Okay, so tea!

My former business partner Nikki Pam handled a lot of administrative duties for Claudia Jordan and through that, I came into the loop of helping with press, bookings and TV projects. When I started working with her, she had just gotten fired from a gig on TV One. We needed to get her back in the spotlight so we could continue getting the bag. We were trying to plan our next move, thinking about what network we could pitch her to. It was a really hectic and dramatic moment, to say the least. Being as connected as I am, I called a former friend, Carlos King, to see if he had a plug or two. I found out that they were casting for another "house wife" to film with Kenya Moore on *Real Housewives*

Of Atlanta. This was during the time she had just had her altercation at the reunion with Porsha, so they wanted a friend on the show for her. It just so happened that he had connections to get her an audition. I suggested to him Claudia. He was apprehensive at first because of her reputation and controversial headlines. I needed some help trying to sell this thing, so my friend, Celebrity Blogger B. Scott and I asked him to at least check her out in person. He agreed to meet us in West Hollywood for drinks at the Abbey. So I told Claudia, "Bitch you better sell it, this can change your entire career!" RHOA was the most watched reality show on cable TV at that time.

Initially she was grateful for the introduction. Even after their initial meeting in West Hollywood that I facilitated, I still privately was pushing for her to get casted - and she did. Personally, I was not expecting anything from her from being casted besides my props in the situation.

However...

(Pour some fresh tea, boo...)

It got rather awkward in the coming months while Claudia filmed RHOA. My business partner ended up helping negotiate her contract, relocate her to Atlanta and actually left her job to assist her during filming. They had their own falling out and naturally, I sided with my business partner because I did see firsthand the work Pam was doing for Claudia, but Claudia saw things differently and felt Pam wanted a come up from her being on the show.

After her one season on RHOA, Claudia and I have had our own spats online and in person, following her public fall out with my business partner. Many people have stepped in and tried to mediate to smooth things out between us, but it reached a boiling point when she was casted for *The Next 15* reality series about former reality stars for TV One.

A lil' more tea...

Carlos King interviewed hundreds of reality stars for the show, but I honestly thought I had it and "this was finally my moment to go back on TV" but it wasn't, thankfully. Prior to the series announcement, I had signed a talent agreement for the series, which was called *Reality Ruined* originally so again, I'm thinking "this is it!" Why would I not be casted? Carlos King had been a close friend to me since I started working in television back in 2006 so if anyone had the power, I assumed it would be him - but nope.

That shit pissed me off. So you know what I did: I shaded the shit out of that show every week it aired on my Twitter feed.

The message in that mess: everything you think is for you, isn't for you. Even though the show's ratings were low and wasn't renewed for a second season, I did get casted a year later for *Love & Hip Hop Hollywood* on Vh1 and have been a regular supporting character since.

While that experience wasn't the best, one of the best experience's was Lisa Raye's event.

Planning Lisa Raye's 50th birthday celebration was an experience all within itself. Bryant McKnight, Lil' Kim, DaBrat and countless other celebrities attended the event in Hollywood and at the time - I had just been physically assaulted in New York during our reunion taping for *Love & Hip Hop* and it was all over TMZ. My full name was in the headline and here I am trying to remain professional while I knew everyone had questions and wanted a first-hand account of what happened.

Lisa Raye is a diva, rightfully so. She has a vision and you're going to see it! This was the first real "PR gig" with a celebrity of this magnitude and demands but my business partner and I were up for the challenge. An added plus was that her daughter Kai and I had been friends years prior and even filmed both seasons of her TV One series "The Real Mccoy" with her so I knew what to expect and how she operates - she runs a tight ship!

When I say this was the most iconic party ever! Chile! Lil Kim arrived at the party, performed on the mic and had the party rocking! My inner gay was stanning while I watched with pride - we did this.

Social Status *did* that!

Now on to the tea!

I really wish I could make this part up, but I can't because this shit really happened. Out of all people who could have shown up to this party, who would have thought it would be Claudia. I know you're probably thinking that it shouldn't be a problem. Well, it was because she came to the party uninvited! Sure did.

My business partner and I sent out the invites and I know I didn't press send on anything attached to her name - so why was she here? She clearly saw the Social Status company logo on the step and repeat beside Ebony Magazine and Ciroc's. But again, why did she show up? I could feel the tension just brewing. Pam was pissed! At least that's what I heard because I was busy, coordinating with security about escorting the arriving celebs to the front section of the party. I saw my business partner making her way through the crowd to confront her and I wish I could have had a front row seat. No hands or drinks were thrown, but words were exchanged, and Claudia was gone.

Despite the drama in the blogs about me on *Love & Hip Hop*, I was still getting to the bag and handling my business. I was mentally exhausted from trying to remain unbothered by the events that happened just 48 hours prior, but I had to keep it pushing. That was one of the most powerful lessons I've had in my life - to keep moving despite the drama.

Lessons As An Entrepreneur

The first lesson I learned as an entrepreneur is that it's scary. Because there's no true stability, you have to quickly learn to put your business first and always be professional. I learned that if you don't get up and go get it, you're not gonna get anything. You are your PTO and 401k. Running a business is nothing like having a nine to five. There's no snow day or sick day. If you don't work, there's no money coming in. So, you're always in the goal mode. This means you need to have more than one project or business popping off or else you're fucked.

So, if I had to share some advice or tips, I would say invest in yourself. There's a saying in business, "You have to have skin in the game." This means you have to be willing to use your own money before making more money. I think that's a big misconception that people have about starting a business. They think it's free. Tuh! It's not. You'll have to pay for the trademark and the logo, marketing and adverting, domains, graphics, the merchandise - just all the little things that go into building a successful business.

Walking The Walk

It's real cute to say that you're a business owner when you're not actually conducting the business. There's so much that goes into having your own business that it can be a little overwhelming. I mean, no one really goes around telling people the ups and downs of their business. They usually only share the wins, so when a new entrepreneur jumps into this game, they do what I did — assume.

Yep, I assumed a lot and learned a lot as well. One thing I learned is that if I talk the talk, I better walk the walk. And for me, being on television and then doing PR, was a little contradicting. See, my job was to represent other people and make them look good. Make sure their brands are being positively marketed. Yet here I am acting an ass on *Love & Hip Hop*! Do you know I had to explain my behavior for the times I didn't display myself on TV in that the best manner?

Embarrassing!

It was a very humbling lesson for me. You know I love to show off, be loud and act a fool, but you can't do that when you're working with high-profile clients. I had to make a choice: do I want to turn up for the camera or do I want people to take me seriously and pay me? Since I wanted people to take me seriously and pay me, I had some changes to make.

During the filming of *Love & Hip Hop*, my business caught a lot of flack. There was a catch twenty-two. On one hand, I started getting exposure. On the other hand, people started associating my logo with drama and that was so frustrating! I didn't want people thinking that if they attend any of my events, there will be food and drinks flying around or waist trainers being snatched. I had to start giving people disclaimers before working with me! The nerve of it all!

Chapter 6

Finding Me

"It's easy to hear the voices of others and often very difficult to hear your own. Every person you meet is going to want something different from you. The question is: what do you want for yourself?"

– *Beyonce*

Whew chile! If someone would have told me that my life would have been a rollercoaster ride after diving into these Hollywood streets I don't know if I would have followed through with coming to Hollywood in the first place. So much happened to me that I begin to lose myself.

It's 2010 and to be honest, I didn't really have a solid backup plan, so I was just doing what I had to do. I had a bunch of odd jobs but nothing that I was passionate about. I was making sure I kept my name and face out there. I was still networking. It was starting to feel like it was a never-ending hustle. Like, every day it was let me wake up and go to this event. So, I can see if I meet someone network or see if I can request someone I know and see if they know of anything going on. And I just got burned out from trying to just hustle and find the next thing like I just got tired of it. I didn't feel like I was accomplishing anything. I didn't feel like I was moving forward. I wasn't really happy with myself. I was drinking and partying way too much. I just was lost. I didn't know what was next for me.

You ever heard of people saying they hit rock bottom? Well, that's exactly how I felt. I needed to climb back to the top but didn't know how to do that. Hollywood was starting to feel really small, and I needed to get away. I remember telling my grandmother that I was gonna go to Atlanta to visit a friend. He was actually a guy that I was talking to at the time, who I hadn't met yet. You can imagine how that went down. It was a whole hot ass mess and once it was over, I decided to stay in Atlanta. I still wasn't ready to go back to Hollywood, so I made a life for myself in Atlanta. I moved in with a friend and started working for a production company. I eventually got my own place and was just, you know, living in Atlanta. I did that for about year before I realized that I still wasn't happy. I woke up one day and I was like, *this isn't it down here either.*

You know, when you're growing through life, it's so hard to make decisions that you feel will be best for you. You kind of have to go through the motions until you really get to the root of your issue. And that's what I did. After a lot of thinking, I decided that it would probably be best for me to go home. I had to be honest with myself and admit that I needed to be around my dad. I needed some structure, and I didn't have that. So, I went back to my comfort zone to be around people I know who love and support me wholeheartedly. Hard, but very necessary decision.

Ray Works Where?

Moving back to Virginia meant going back to a regular life. That meant that I needed to get a j-o-b. I knew that my dad wasn't going to play around with me being lazy or not working a stable job, so I got a job – at Amtrak. I did not want to get a job, and especially not at Amtrak. I'm a star, honey! I belong on the tube! Okay, just kidding, but seriously, I wasn't feeling working for Amtrak at first. My dad kept saying to me that I needed stability. He'd tell me repeatedly to get a regular job with a schedule and benefits. Even though I did *not* want to hear any of what he had to say, he was right.

So, I didn't hesitate when I moved home to apply for Amtrak.

Now, my father is an Amtrak alumnus, and do you know I still had to apply? I couldn't even get the hookup! I had to do everything everyone else did. I had to submit an application, go through interview process, physical tests and drug test, waiting for them to call back and send paperwork and waiting for her to go through orientation – the whole nine. My dad has clout at Amtrak, so it was a gift and a curse to work for the same company. Once the initial shock wore off, I was just another employee trying to get my coins and move up the ranks. Unfortunately, since my dad was basically superman at Amtrak, I had some big shoes to fill. Also, the company didn't want to seem like I'm getting a pass because of my father so you know, they were a little more tough on me than the others. I didn't let that bother me, though. I was in my own world doing my own thing.

You know how I do!

It didn't take long for me to find some eye candy to help make this job a lot more fun.

Okay so tea. Now, the railroad is a very masculine industry. It's also a very white-male industry. So, when my Black, gay ass, joined the company, I was definitely shaking things up. I didn't go in looking to get into anything. Hell, I never do. So, when I met one of the managers of a different crew base, I gave him some play. And play did we! We had a good time, too. So much so that at one point, he was riding with me, on his off days. So yes, I was secretly enjoying being on the train. There were definitely some whispers and some rumblings about my love riding with me, but no one said anything to me. Well, my manager directly questioned me about it. And she basically told me that fraternizing with co-workers was frowned upon at the company. And that's all she said about it.

So yep, that was definitely an interesting experience. But with everything else, it was time for me to move on from Amtrak. Now, I have to say this, I actually liked working for Amtrak. The last two years of my employment, they actually had me on a special assignment. I was traveling to different cities and states representing the company attempting to get more African American ridership. They also wanted to get more HBCU students on the train, and because I was an HBCU graduate, that was my qualification to fulfill that assignment. The downfall transpired after being promised a promotion and never being considered for the position. And you know I wasn't feeling that! Especially since I was being sent out to do the work and someone else was getting the credit for it and being paid for it. I got tired of being lied to. Tired of being strung along for my contacts to benefit them. I was getting nothing out of it but trips to Charlotte, New York, Chicago, and Los Angeles. I loved every minute, okay! But I wasn't getting anything more out of it. It wasn't anything rewarding for me.

Then I got mad.

I thought, *I could be doing this myself, I can be working with the school, working with these clients, and doing this for myself.* So I decided to do just that. I was like, *I'm gonna go back to LA, and I'm going to restart my company. I'm going to reach out to all my old clients, see if they need anything, and just start working. And hopefully this works out for the best.* And that's how I did it. And I left.

Now, don't let me get you to thinking it was easy because it was not! It was scary because I know I had some competition. I was going to have to put in the work all over again, but that wasn't a problem for me. I just didn't want to fail, you know. Since I technically never stopped working in the industry, I had enough confidence to follow through with my thoughts.

Oh, you thought I was done stunting?

Nope, I just put my talent on the shelf while I regroup and come up with a fire strategy to get back in the game and win.

So yeah, I was doing outside work while I was working with Amtrak. I was actually working at a TV station in Qatar. I also worked at the local radio, as I was doing the entertainment news for their morning show. In addition to that, I was a correspondent for Roland Martin's show, News One, on TV one. And I was doing Good Morning, Washington.

So, I was working, okay! But not in the capacity that I wanted so I had to dip out on Amtrak. After chopping it up with God about my next move, I went for it. I threw up a "Please Lord give me a sign", prayer asking for confirmation that going back to L.A. was the right thing for me to do and I took that leap, again.

Going Back To Cali

Going back to California was definitely nerve wracking for me because I had been in DC for about five years. So, I had friends, I had a circle there. I established myself there. I was the name of the city with me, I was made for DC. I was comfortable there; I had a routine I was able to get down to Virginia to see my family for different little family events and occasions. And now here I am leaving all that to go cross country to Los Angeles, for something not very promising if I have to add.

I was leaving behind familiarity, to a place where I only had my mother and my grandmother. And to be honest, I really didn't have a relationship with my mother at the time, so it was a very uncomfortable decision. But a very necessary one for me if I really want to pursue my dreams.

Listen, I was so nervous about this move. I was going out there with no job in place, no projects lined up, just going! All I had was a place to lay my head. In terms of getting a coin, nothing was concrete. You ever heard the phrase, *Walk by faith, not by sight?* Well, that's what I was doing because I didn't see a dollar sign in sight! I just believed that there was more for me, and I was using my faith to get there.

Now, I may not have had a job or project lined up, but ya boy definitely had a plan. I was good at networking, I'm talented and hardworking. Something would pop off. I told myself that I was going to make this work, by any means necessary, you hear me? I was not about to have another one of those "I told you so" conversations with my dad.

No ma'am, no sir!

So, here I am. Not a damn thing confirmed. But I still went.

Best. Decision. *Ever.*

Chapter 7

LA: Round Two

"Step out of the history that is holding you back. Step into the new story you are willing to create."

- *Unknown*

After I got settled in California, I was ready to get to work and reintroduce myself. So, I started grinding and utilizing every resource and blessing on layaway I had. My grind knew no stranger, if you worked with me or worked with someone, I knew directly I was following up with you about any new leads with working in the office, behind the camera or on-air. I had only been back in LA for about three months, and I get a phone call from casting for *Love & Hip Hop*. Come to find out my girlfriend Nia Riley who's Teddy Riley's daughter and ex-girlfriend of Soulja Boy had recommended me to casting and they were interested in me joining the cast. I was here for it! It came out of the blue, but I was ready for whatever that would benefit my career, in a good way of course. But yes, I got the call and to be honest, I just knew I was going to get the part. Although I had to audition it was just something that sat in my spirit that confirmed this is for me. Luckily for me, I was very much resurrected already and visible on WEtv's network. I hosted and executive produced their award-winning digital weekly series *Reality Wrap* recapping *Braxton Family Values, LA Hair, Growing Up*

Hip Hop, SWV: Reunited and *Cutting It ATL* which ran for six years, created and hosted the networks digital awards The Realities and my dream came true when I was green-lit to host my own digital talk show series, 100 & Real with Misster Ray for them as well. I didn't even audition yet before I started telling my friends that I was going to be on *Love & Hip Hop*. I guess you can say that I was speaking it into existence. And that's exactly what I did because shortly after, my sister received a phone call about me being a part of the show.

Just the possibility of being considered was enough for me, so I was truly excited. I always said to myself that if I ever did reality TV again, it would have to be bigger than what I've already done. I mean, what's bigger than *Love & Hip Hop?* Exactly! So, I wasn't passing up this opportunity. I was determined as ever to make it my second go round in LA. I was smarter, wiser and surer of my brand. I knew what kind of representation I wanted, I knew what circles I wanted to be in, I knew what I needed to avoid to stay focused.

The conversation with the producer was so easy it was hard to pass up. It just felt natural to talk about the people and things we talked about. And I wasn't having to make up anything because I did work in Hollywood. I lived in Hollywood, I had friends in Hollywood, I had drama in Hollywood. I dated in Hollywood; I partied in Hollywood. I saw a lot and I knew a lot that was going on in Hollywood. It wasn't a stretch. There was nothing created or manufactured. It was natural. I went in thinking that everything was going to change for the better. My name is gonna be back out there. This is gonna be a whole new world of opportunities. Being in the age of social media, I knew the possibilities would be endless. When I filmed *College Hill* there was no Facebook, Twitter, Instagram or TikTok. It was literally just Myspace. I'm always at a loss for words when I meet younger people who "remember" me and tell me they were inspired by *College Hill* to go to college, specifically my season. So, there was a whole new audience, a whole new generation that was going to be introduced to me as Misster Ray.

The final interview audition for *Love &
Hip Hop* was intense - all the executives were
sitting around the table with Mona at the
head like the queen she is. She was very
direct and kept a straight face for the
majority of the interview and with every
question they asked, I knew I was hilarious
and quick witted - it was crickets and head
nods only! I didn't know if they thought I
was funny or not. I decided to sign the talent
agreement and contract to be a part of the
cast for season four. Here I am making my
grand return to television with Keyshia
Cole, Brooke Valentine, Bridgette Kelly,
Boobie Gibson and Alexis Sky who were also
new cast members as well. I was excited, too.
I was ready for the positive changes, but not
so much for the backlash and negativity.
What I thought would be a dream started to
feel like a nightmare. It became drama filled
and I didn't like that but once I realized this
was a job and took my personal feelings out
of the equation, now it's a breeze and
thankful to Mona Scott-Young for the
opportunity.

Being a reality star has it's fun
moments, but it also comes with moments

filled with anxiety, depression, nervousness, and lots of shade, honey. It comes with lies, rumors, and everything that I did not expect. And I had to basically suck it up and deal with it. I mean, it comes with the territory so either deal with or walk away. I decided to deal with it per se because it was what I wanted. Things started out great, but then it took a shift. Just as I was starting to adjust to being in the spotlight, a bitch starts going bald!

Chapter 8

Headlines & Hollywood Tea

You can have all the degrees in the world but if you don't have a hustler's mentality, ambition, & common sense you'll be lost.

– Jay Z

I will say this, having alopecia played a huge role in the feuds I had on the show. I just didn't know I had alopecia at the time, so it made my life a little stressful. I was diagnosed with Alopecia areata multilocularis which refers to multiple areas of hair loss. That's why you probably saw me on WEtv and *Love & Hip Hop* looking like a bloated, hardboiled egg with absolutely *no* facial hair or edges, much less hair. The first symptoms I experienced were small bald patches. The underlying skin is unscarred and looks normal. Although these patches can take many shapes, they are usually round or oval. Alopecia areata most often affects the scalp and beard but may occur on any part of the body with hair. Different areas of the skin may exhibit hair loss and regrowth at the same time. The disease may also go into remission for a time or may be permanent.

When I first learned about alopecia, I had no clue what it was. I just knew that my hair started thinning and I started freaking the hell out. At first I was thinking, *Oh, it must be the sulfate in this Pantene Pro-V for women*. That's what I was using at the time. So I rationalized it with that. The sulfate is super, super strong, and it's breaking my hair off. But then also I remembered the time I used to dye my hair a lot as well. Auburn, blonde or jet black, whatever I was feeling, you know? I always wanted to dye my hair in high school, but my stepmother wouldn't let me. So, me being rebellious at the time would dye my hair when I'd visit my family for the summers in L.A. I should have slowed down because I begin to notice that my hair was thinning. Well, one of those summers didn't go so well. I went and got green contacts, dyed my hair blonde, and proceeded to live my life.

Listen! I put that mess in my hair and do you know my hair fell out! I was in the shower, washing my hair and it was just coming out like water. I could see it in my hands. I could see it lying around my toes. I immediately thought, *oh my God, I got cancer or something!* I didn't know what was going on, but I knew that something was wrong.

And I was scared.

I didn't say anything to my family about it at first because I honestly didn't know how to mention it. So I kept it hidden, that is until it was so noticeable that they couldn't deny asking *me* about it. One day I went to the barber and was like, "My hair is coming out, bro. I don't know what's wrong. It's thinning." He said, "Well, let's just try to cut it and make it even all over and then we'll see what we got." By time he made it even and cut it down, my hair was so thin and so fine. It looked like I was bald headed!

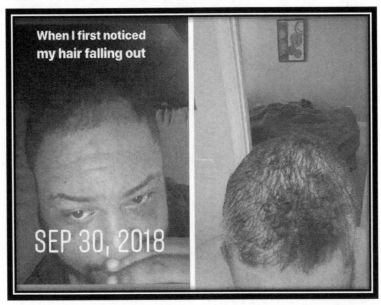

I didn't know how to feel. At first I got pissed off at the barber. In my mind, *I was*

like, this nigga just messed my hair up! He cut off all my hair and I told him I wanted a fade. In my mind, I'm blaming him, I even stopped going to him and everything. I'm looking all crazy and it's his fault. Still, I didn't address it or ask anyone else about it. Instead I did what most Black men do when their hair starts thinning: I started wearing lots of hats.

I continued to ignore the fact that my hair was thinning and focused on my career. But that became hard after I noticed the hair on other areas on my body was also starting to thin. One day, I noticed that my beard was looking a little different. I had a full beard when I went to bed. Then I woke up the next day and I had a patch of hair missing in my beard. Yep, you read that correctly. I had a damn bald spot in my beard. I'm looking at myself in the mirror like, *What is this? Did I get drunk? Did I chew some gum, and it got stuck in it? Did I do this myself? Did I shave it off by accident?* I was trying to recall my night because there has to be a reason why I'm looking crazy right now. I ran my hand over the patch, and it was smooth. That alarmed me. It was like there was no hair there ever.

There was no stubble. It was nothing. So, I'm looking at the bed, I'm looking down on the floor, looking at the sheet. I'm trying to see if some of my hair fell out in the bed. Like, I should have seen something, but I didn't see anything.

I still didn't go to the doctor to see what the issue was. Instead, I switched it up, cut my beard off and just kept a goatee. I told myself that I'll let it regrow. Then I noticed that my beard wasn't growing back. Then I started noticing little patches in my eyebrows. I'm known for having my eyebrows, freshly threaded. That was my pride and joy: having some good eyebrows. And of course I thought the lady who did my eyebrows was trying to fuck 'em up. She was like, "No. It looks like you don't have any hair growing right there." And she was right. It was a small patch on my right eyebrow. And eventually, that same patch appeared in the left one. And then my eyebrows started thinning all together.

So now at this point, I have no beard. I barely have a goatee. My mustache has not even fully grown yet. I'm looking like

Chester the molester. I looked weird and it began to affect my self-esteem. After complaining to my sister about it, she told me to go to the doctor. So, I went to a dermatologist and that's when I learned that I had alopecia.

Okay, so what exactly is alopecia? It's basically a battle within your body and because it's effects your immune system, it causes your hair follicles to fall out. It's actually something that can be inherited. So once I understood that I tried to get it remedied, but then I got super busy. It was time for me to start filming *Love & Hip Hop*.

This came with mixed emotions. I was hella excited to be on this show, but I was hella nervous because I didn't have any hair on my face. What was I going to do? Go on TV looking a mess?

Thank God I didn't have to. I lie to you not. I got that contract in December of 2016. My hair started growing January 2017. Listen! God knew I didn't want to be on TV looking a mess and He made sure I was straight. How's **THAT** for a message!

So yeah, in January I started noticing facial hair sprouting up again and my eyebrows were growing back. My overly extensive Google search paid off. Baby, I was googling everything online to get this hair growing. I was buying Jamaican castor oil. I was buying raw castor oil. I was buying any kind of oil that Google said will make your hair grow and doing what the internet said. My hair, beard, and eyebrows grew in enough for me to be confident enough to be myself on air.

Unfortunately, that didn't last too long.

During my second season of the show, I noticed my hair started to thin again. One of my friends pointed it out one day. She asked, "Did you wake up from a nap?" I'm like, "Why?" She said, "The back of your hair looks like a cow licked it." And sure enough, bald spots were starting to form again. I'm thinking, oh my God. I can't film the show like this. With the patches being in the back of my head mad it hard to disguise. There was no hat that could save me from the embarrassment I felt. So I did what most

Black men who are avoiding this issue does: I got braids.

Alopecia is the only reason I had those braids. And to be honest, braids are the last thing that I should have gotten. The traction from the braids and putting them in different hairstyles did more damage. When I took those braids out, I had patches of hair missing in my braids. I'd wake up one morning with two braids in my bed. Then it was three. And the next time it was four. My hair was starting to literally just snap off and fall out. I didn't want to tell anyone about what I was going through because, I mean, I was ashamed. Plus, I didn't want people assuming lies about me (we'll talk about that next chapter). So, I took a deep breath and shared my truth about battling with alopecia. And then...

What In The Alopecia?

Now, I'm already an emotional wreck about my hair and overall appearance, but I still had to work so I had to go through with showing up on set, even though I wasn't feeling it. I just heard that my grandmother had cancer, now the rest of the cast is giving me the side-eye because they're starting to question why I have on this hat all of the time. I started to feel my world caving in on me and I just broke down. I remember meeting with one of the producers of the show. I didn't even say anything, I just showed her my head. Then I explained to her why I was wearing the hat, and why I was distracted. She held my hand and said, "Okay, we're going to send you home. Go home, go and be with your grandmother. We're going to work out your green screen look." We had a guy come in to shave my head.

I put my hat back on. They beat my face to the gods, and I was ready to work again. She sat in there with me while I did my interviews. I'm forever grateful to her for that.

Now, on to the tea.

After the episode aired and the fans noticed my very drastic look, they dragged my ass from Sunday to Saturday! There I was in a gray suit looking like Dr. Evil. I had no eyebrows, or facial hair. I looked a hot ass mess! I was every meme you could think of. Since I've been diagnosed with alopecia, and I am taking steroids for it, my face is bloated, my body's bloated. And so, on top of me being bald, and hairless, I'm bloated. Okay, let a bitch call a spade a spade: I was fat, okay. And I hate every minute of it.

Everyone knows that my character on the show is kind of over the top and sassy. I'm a little playfully messy. But I had to keep it a buck with myself and have an Issa Rae, mirror bitch moment, *How are you going to be messy on TV and try to read somebody and you over here with no hair, no eyebrows, no beard, bald head and bloated.* You know what I'm saying? I had to read myself about that. I recall going on my Facebook page and seeing that my appearance was trending. I wasn't trending because I was popular. I was trending because they were joking on how I looked. That hurt my little heart. But not too much because I know that people are people and didn't know what was going on with me. However, I decided to make a statement and let them know what's going on with me and my journey with alopecia.

And then it went viral.

My announcement went everywhere! It was on all the blogs. I even had an alopecia foundation contact me. I had so many celebrities contacting me opening up about their battle with alopecia as well. L.T. Hutton who produced "All Eyes on Me", told me that what I did was empowering. He told me that I was a voice for a lot of people because a lot of people struggle with alopecia, especially Black men. And it's true. They don't ever just own it. And he's the one who actually told me that Tupac had alopecia. Interesting, right? But you know, women with alopecia can wear a wig to cover it up. Black men have a different struggle with this. At the end of the day, your hair is a part of your personality and when you don't feel confident about your hair, it affects other areas of your life.

Having alopecia not only affected my professional life, but also my love life. I was in a very toxic relationship at the time, and he appeared to be supportive of me and my hair journey. However, after we broke up, it got a little ugly online. He posted pictures of me sleeping in my house and in my bed, on my couch, with my hair patches showing. And that hurt me because it wasn't about my hair. My mental health wasn't the best and he didn't protect me. There were times I just was too emotionally drained to shave my hair; I was too drunk to shave my head, or I got too high to shave my head. I was just trying to numb myself in every which way because I did not like how I looked at all. My life was spiraling out of control, and I was just so lost. I didn't know what to do about anything anymore. My cast members, the fans, and now the man I *thought* I loved were all attacking me. I was just done! I remember thinking that the Lord is trying to give me a sign to let me know that this isn't supposed to be my life. If that was the case, then, I was ready to give it up.

After another online altercation, I said, *I get it, Lord, I get it.* I've done got knock upside my head, I've got called every name, I've been attacked and now I've even lost my hair. I took the sign and decided that I mentally need a break from Hollywood.

No Shade, No Shame

If there's one thing that I want Black men to understand about alopecia is that they are not alone. Once I shared my hair diagnosis, so many Black men were messaging me about their hair struggles as well and identified with my story of being diagnosed. Many of them were wearing hats or just shaved their heads bald completely and just wrote it off as "it's expected" as a man but it's not. Alopecia Areata is common in Black men, more than 70% are affected with it. A lot of hair styles Black men wear such as locs, braids, and cornrows directly trigger hair loss and can be damaging if he's undiagnosed with having alopecia. And because we don't talk about it, of course these men don't know not to wear these hairstyles. I mean, their culturally accepted so it's natural for them to want to. We just have to find other styles for men suffering with suffering and also educate them more.

Which is why I started PRISM.

Yes, I'm plugging my new business. Who gon' check me boo?!

So, PRISM is my new business baby, and I'm very excited to introduce this product to the Black community. While on my hair journey, I was inspired to create a hair product of my own based on me trying various products over the last three years and researching hair growth practices. After going viral for my announcement and shocking appearance on television, I decided to infuse all the hero ingredients of the various products together that worked best for me and of course, consulted with a dermatologist to create PRISM. You'd be surprised to know about the things you expose your sensitive skin to on a daily basis because you're looking for just those hero ingredients and those sometimes get mixed in with a bunch of other things that are necessarily good for us. I didn't know any of this stuff and honestly had I not dealt with Alopecia I probably might still not know but here I am more aware of what's going on and how to improve my symptoms and manage my own diagnosis.

Through conversations with my medical team, I shared with them the products I was using. We carefully and tediously went through each product, and they informed me of the pros and cons of each ingredient.

I've created the Hair Glow Collection and have been using it for several months now and I've seen some pretty amazing results. My hair has grown back healthier, fuller, thicker, softer, curlier and even some grey hairs, okay! I don't care what color my hair grows back as, I got my edges back!

Oh, you think I'm capping? Check ya boy out on the 'Gram. This hair is giving what's it's supposed to give.

Okay, seriously, this product is amazing and those who are battling with Alopecia really need to get into it. Now, although I created this product with Black men in mind, PRISM is for everyone in the spotlight that deals with Alopecia and are struggling with getting those bald spots filled and edges back. We're all being watched whether we know it or not! When the spotlight hits you, I want everyone to be confident and let their true light shine. The same way prism breaks light into beautiful colors, I want people to use my PRISM product to help restore their **GLOW**. Shine baby!

Oh, and by the way…

Alopecia Areata is *not* contagious! It has been proven, but it's believed to be heredity.

I know you probably have tons of questions about this disease, so I personally reached out to the National Alopecia Areata Foundation at <u>NAAF.ORG</u> for support and information. They provide local groups, contacts and events for support and are persistent with sending information on literature and various study's available.
But yeah…

It's pretty difficult to find a common treatment for it since there hasn't been a known-common factor that triggers the disease. So, it's possible that the hair may regrow in many cases. It can be a stressful process because you know, you're taking the time and spending money on products hoping for this to work and it's possible that it won't. Personally for me, I was willing to try any and everything to get my edges back! I took the risk. I felt and I was extremely depressed and didn't want to feel that way anymore. You couldn't tell me I didn't look unattractive, which lead to my involvement in toxic relationships with people based on me being insecure. The steroids bloated me, and the creams irritated my scalp, eventually making it super sensitive and tender at times.

After beating myself up over my looks and getting out of those toxic relationships, I decided to do something about my hair. I used a variety of healthy hair products that promoted hair repair and regrowth as well as changed my diet to nearly gluten-free.

There's no tea on this, but the message: I consider myself blessed and lucky to have had the hair regrowth I've had. I know that anytime, it could return so I try to avoid associated triggers like stress and just remain grateful for this moment, whether I'm bad or rocking this beautiful curly fro' of mine.

Okay, maybe that's a little *iced* tea...

Chapter 9

New Number, Who This?

"I Am No Longer Accepting The Things I Cannot Change. I Am Changing The Things I Cannot Accept."

-Unknown

Listen! I am so grateful for new beginnings. That is the one thing that God has shown me over and over again. No matter how many times I fail, experience pain, or feel defeated, I can always have a new beginning. And that's where I am in my life right now, experiencing many new beginnings. So many new opportunities have been pouring in and I know it's because I'm open to receive all things new, especially new money!

Okay, now I am not about to brag about what's going on in my world. I'm just sharing these wins because of all of the losses I've experienced during my low moments. You know, when you're down and out, you're still dreaming. Dreaming of the house you want to live in, or the car you want to drive, or the spouse you want to be boo'd up with. So when you start receiving these things, you naturally want to share. For whatever reason, people think it's bragging, when really I'm just proud of my accomplishments and grateful for the blessing. Anyway, I'm sharing because I want you to know that you too can win again after losing. Fantasia has a song that says,

"Sometimes you gotta lose to win again." I understand that phrase so much right now!

Okay, so this is like, some *business* tea. We sip that over here, too! Here's what's new with me.

I was blessed to be able to do something amazing. I created a board game! Yep, a real-life board game, honey! It's called YARD U and it's truly my legacy and passion project. After I had wrapped production in the fall of 2017, I started finding different ways to keep myself entertained and learning. I remember coming across all these various Opoly-games in Barnes & Nobles. They were specialty board games that were collector items prices but had nothing that appealed or was marketed towards the African-American demographic. I love a good board game, and so does many of the people I associate with. I thought, *I need something like this in my life.* So I started looking for a game that I could relate to. I had to search in five different stores to get Steve Harvey's *Family Feud* game for our annual holiday sweater party in Virginia. And who has time to do all of that whenever they want a new game? Not me!

I really loved the concept of having a specialty board game that caters to people who look like me. So me being the creative that I am, I said I want to make a board game celebrating HBCU's since I am the product of one. I thought I can pay homage to my *College Hill* experience, which spiked enrollment and inspired a generation of HBCU graduates. There are so many people who have no clue about the history of these staple institutions. Many of them never heard of a HBCU until they saw Beyonce's Coachella Homecoming HBCU-themed performance. With people often asking me what the experience is like, I thought the game would be a perfect way to explain that. I mean, my HBCU experience at Virginia State University changed my life, my entire senior year is forever documented and available on every streaming app. Yep, I can pay homage for that.

So, while planning the idea of YARD U was fun, bringing it to life was work! Over a two-year period, I went through numerous consultations with lawyers and HBCU affiliated sponsors about bringing YARD U to life. You know, I had to make sure I had the legalities in order. I don't need any problems, okay! I learned most of these schools don't own their trademark (name, logo, mascot etc.) so I had to be careful and creative with bringing the ultimate HBCU experience to life.

I didn't realize a board game has so many components to it and it really took almost 7-9 months figuring out the board theme, how the players would navigate collecting 120 college credits by the end of the fourth time around the board (senior year) to graduate. Even down to determining the majors available for the game, trivia questions and characters for game were a tedious process but with the help of my graphics designer Kenosha of Flexgraphixs, we laid the foundation for the board game - we just needed to find a home for it, a Black owned one, of course.

We found the perfect company and I was elated. Finally! Something I've been dreaming about and working so hard for is coming into fruition. After we were about to start production of the game, everything fell apart. Spring of 2020 changed my launch date due to the pandemic forcing the manufacturing company to temporarily close. Eventually, they went out of business unfortunately.

While I totally understood that everything was out of all of our controls, I was so disappointed. But God shifted my mind and reminded me that this is delayed, not denied. That made me pause and just be grateful that I was even still able to think about launching a board game, let alone still alive. After checking myself, I regrouped. I was able to refocus on the game more and found a Black owned game manufacturing company called In All Seriesness, which produced The Hillman game inspired by the 80s sitcom *A Diff'rent World* created by Bill Cosby. So I'm super excited to introduce the game to the world.

YARD U isn't just for HBCU graduates, just to be clear. It's for the culture. Yard U was created to celebrate historically Black colleges and universities as well as unite generations of HBCU alumni and supporters. This board game being the first of its kind will celebrate Black education, our history and culture. The first edition "HBCU 101" is presented by Fairfax Studios, so shout to them. And well, developing this game actually inspired me to do something else: I went back to school.

Grad School Here I Come!

So, the apocalypse, I mean, when the pandemic hit - I was visiting my best friend Cameron in Atlanta and had absolutely no money coming in because we weren't able to film. With the contract I had, I was not legally able to film anything for any other network. Here I am again, unemployed and unknowing of when I would even return to filming. I'm just going to keep it real with you. After I was done creating YARD U, I had way too much time on my hands so after wasting a whole year due to the pandemic I decided I would use the time to further my education. I've always talked about going back to school but due to filming and other life obligations, I just didn't have the time. Now, I had the chance to finally get my masters, so I took that chance. So glad that I did! Of course I went back to Virginia State

University. I'll be majoring in Media Management. I finished my first semester in the spring of 2021 with a 3.5 GPA and have an expected December 2022 graduation date. Can I tell you that I am beyond excited? I mean, of course I've been in media all of my adult life for reality tv drama but to now be mentioned as an "notable HBCU alumni" returning to school was so affirming and positive for my supporters to see. To see others enthusiasm about me taking the next steps to really hone my craft excites me. It's not always easy for adults to go back to school. Hell, we have bills! We don't have time to be writing essays and turning in online homework. We want to take naps and tequila shots! It wasn't easy for me to do this, but it was necessary. I couldn't have done this without the support of my family, friends and campus community. To them, I'm truly appreciative.

Now, having said all of that…

Brand New

The saying that 'You can't teach an old dog new tricks' isn't true because this old dog has learned a new trick or two. I've been out of college since 2006, which means it's been fifteen years since I have been in school, had a notebook, books, took a test or wrote a paper – yet I'm doing it. I felt old and out of place yet determined to do this program. Since 2006, I've had extensive hands-on job experience within that field and now with me doing more talent management and more upper-level corporate PR, I thought that me getting my master's in media management was the correct thing to do in terms of me having longevity in this industry.

I've always been on the thick side, so I never wanted to be super skinny, but when I saw myself looking like a walking hard broiled egg, I knew something needed to be done. But can I be honest? Even though I felt ugly, that wasn't enough to make me get up and lose weight. I gained pandemic weight just like everyone else, but that still didn't force me to lose it. My weight loss journey started because I was undiagnosed and was untreated for hypoglycemia, which is a complication of diabetes, and it means that my body does not produce sugar regularly. Diabetes does run in my family on both sides and as I'm getting older I decided to start going to the doctor and getting regular checkups. Well, I went to the doctor because my hormones were all out of whack. I was having some pretty bad headaches and these hangry outburst were coming left and right. Come to find out my mother also suffers from hypoglycemia, and she identified the symptoms in me through her which prompted me to go to the doctor to figure out what was the best way to combat this in reverse the diagnosis. I have had several medical scares where the paramedics had to be called due to my blood sugar dropping extremely low which resulted in me fainting literally where I stood. Thankfully, I'd always be with my friends. With all that being said I had to learn how to eat right from my blood type as well as maintaining a healthy balanced diet and exercise and all of these positive changes I truly feel contributed to my hair restoration and regrowth.

What's the Message in this Mess?

This is me - no edits, true tea. My best advice to everyone is to pass the plate and sip the juice like we do in church! I've learned through all of this, what I cannot control - give it up and turn it loose! Or as my dad always says, identify the problem and give it to the source. I often relate my life to the biblical story of the prodigal son. I lost my way, went after what I wanted, didn't necessarily get the results I desired and was welcomed back home. Adapting, improvising and overcoming has been my formula to my success in life.

Chapter 10

New Attitude

"If you work hard and meet your responsibilities, you can get ahead, no matter where you come from, what you look like, or who you love."

– Barack Obama

Prior to the pandemic and after I had returned from Atlanta to film our reunion, I found out from the landlord she had settled her divorce and was selling the townhouse in Woodland Hills, CA. It's the end of the year and I literally had less than 30 days to move. Our show checks were coming in but with no definite schedule and I wasn't prepared to move that sudden. I was in a rapid downward spiral in my personal life and needed a change of scenery immediately or I wouldn't be here writing this memoir. Life started to kick my ass and get the best of me. My recreational drug use and alcohol binges were starting to become my norm. I was over indulging in everything to self-medicate due to feeling depressed about having alopecia and feeling "ugly". Everything in my life was toxic and I was beginning to see these people, circumstances, and situations were blocking my blessings. It was clear I needed to make some changes personally before I could do anything else professionally. Thankfully my college friend Marcy identified the signs of me asking for help and she without asking bought me a flight to Atlanta to visit my best friend Cameron, not knowing within 24 hours Covid-19 would change all of our lives and the way we live forever.

California's numbers were alarmingly sky high and I wasn't taking any changes. I honestly wasn't in any rush to go back to Los Angeles. This was the break I mentally needed after the 2019 I had. So for the entire pandemic I stayed in Atlanta, but I didn't see things first hand besides the face mask regulations and limited Uber's available. While the rest of the world was dealing with unemployment and the election race between Trump vs Biden - Atlanta was fully **OPEN**! Hookah bars, clubs, restaurants, museums etc. Wasn't nothing closed in Atlanta! I was outside while the rest of the world was at home and as irresponsible as it looked, I did always keep a mask on. Thankfully, I never had Covid-19 and am fully vaccinated with Pfizer.

Going Back To Cali

Being in Atlanta for the majority of the pandemic was peaceful for me and a time to reflect, refocus and realign myself with my purpose. A YouTube series called *You Hittin Dat?* created by Juhahn Jones and directed by Dame Pierre was being made into a film, *You Married Dat???* also co-starting my *Love & Hip Hop Hollywood* cast mate Apryl Jones. My character was introduced in 2018 during the first season with over 1 million views for the episode and twice again during the second season in 2019.

My anxiety didn't hit until I was preparing to fly back to LA in November to film my scenes. Was I ready to be back in LA? I haven't seen anyone, are they going to judge me for leaving so quickly without an explanation as to why? I was all in my own head and stressing myself out. Needless to say, I killed my scenes and delivered my lines to the best of my ability. The film is coming out summer 2021 and I officially add this to my resume: **ACTOR**. What was really sitting heavy on my mind was my non-existent and toxic relationship with my mother. I wasn't looking forward to being anywhere remotely near her at the time. My grandmother was turning 89 and I didn't want to be in the wrong headspace going into filming my first movie. Once again, it was about me clearing the air so I could function normally because I can't do consistent drama - it stresses me out.

Forgiveness Set Me Free

I honestly do not know how things with my mother would go because we hadn't spoken during the pandemic much less prior to the pandemic and before that the last time we spoke was when my roommate stayed to intervene for me because things were spiraling down word very fast for me. My mother did not know where I was living, what state I was in or where the car was parked when the pandemic started and never bothered to check up and see which further fueled my frustrations and hatred towards her. My grandmother's only request for a birthday wish was that I speak to her and try to make things right as for Mimi. I did that not knowing that I needed it for myself more than I knew. I didn't get emotional about reconnecting with my mother on my grandmother's birthday until after I left, and I didn't realize how much of a void was in my life and how impactful her absence was in my life. As the saying goes you only get one love you and this is very true but dammit I didn't have a choice and I wasn't understanding why my relationship with my mother and my stepmother was the way it was. Two of

the most important women in my life, I
didn't get along with, so I had to figure out
what was wrong with me as well because it
wasn't all just them... most of it, not all of it.

In recent years and as I have grown
older I have been able to accept what was
and move on to work and have sent it to
build a better relationship with my
stepmother and mother and it has proven to
be therapeutic in a de-stressor for me in
terms of my mental health. I have I have not
forgotten anything that has been done to me
or said to me in my childhood teenage in the
years but I'm also not dwelling on them
everybody goes through things in their life
which caused us to react and respond a
certain kind of way and it's up to us if we
hold on and live by those words and I refused
to live by anything that was told to me
negatively and I enjoy proving people
wrong.

Grateful For It All

I've heard the phrase, "Your attitude
determines your altitude" more times than I
care to remember. While I may have not

understood what it meant the first time, I for sure understand what it means now. Because I allowed God to work on my attitude, the opportunities for me have been endless. And although I would never want to repeat the year 2020, it was the catalyst for the shift within me.

Who would have thought that the world could come to an almost standstill while we all try to stay safe and sane. I surely didn't but I'm actually grateful for it. Though sad, it had a deeper purpose for all mankind. We all had the opportunity to reflect. And that's exactly what I did. I realize that my experience with alopecia was confirmation that I need to get back to who Misster Ray is and why Misster Ray even came back to Hollywood. Worrying about my hair is such a small thing when thinking about the plans that God has for my life. I'm so grateful that I've been able to rediscover myself – and that's all thanks to COVID.

To be honest, I probably would still be doing fuck shit if the world didn't shut down in 2020. I could complain about COVID, and having alopecia, but I needed that season. I needed that year to regroup, refocus and realign myself. To learn how to properly love myself. I've been able to do a lot of growing, healing, and it stemmed from me being embarrassed of my appearance and being stuck in the house, which I now appreciate. It forced me to look deeper than my resume and accolades. *What do I want to do with my life? What type of legacy do I want to leave?* I mean, I come from a very legendary family, so I need to make sure my greatness is established. I realized that I couldn't do that with the mindset that I was in pre-COVID.

Now I'm able to openly share my hair journey on my platform. I eat better, I'm taking better care of myself. Not drinking and smoking as much or eating fast food. I'm drinking my water. I'm learning that it's okay to be sober and that I don't have to get super drunk to enjoy myself.

Although I'm officially back in these Hollywood streets, I'm a smarter, wiser man now. I understand the importance of staying true to myself and keeping God first in my life. I can honestly say that I'm happy now.

Yep, I love it here.

About the Author

If anyone keeps it real, it's Ray Cunningham affectionately known as Misster Ray who is everyone's over the top gay friend in their head with no filter from Virginia. He is a hilariously messy, quick-witted media personality, social media influencer and now talk show host that gives an entertaining spin on trending topics, celebrity culture and social issues.

Misster Ray is a LA-based multimedia maven establishing himself on various platforms including television, radio (WCDX iPower 92 in Virginia & WKYS 93.9 in Maryland) and digital media. He is best known from his ground-breaking television appearance on BET's *College Hill* as the networks first-ever gay on air talent and joined Mona Scott Young's highly successful *Love & Hip Hop* franchise shaking up Hollywood since his debut in 2017 on season four for Vh1.

Easily one of the busiest men in entertainment, he hosted WEtv's first digital talk show series *100 & Real* with Misster Ray and became the award-winning creator/host of WEtv's longest running digital series, *Reality Wrap*; he also the hosted network's annual awards, *The Realies* from 2015-2017.

In addition to his multi-media endeavors, Ray has been awarded for being a successful tastemaker and social media influencer. He is the owner & CEO of Social Status PR. A proud HBCU alumni of Virginia State University, he also started a minority scholarship for mass communications students to assist with financial assistance during summer internships and created Yard U, America's first novelty board game celebrating HBCUs produced by IAS Games, LLC.

Made in the USA
Columbia, SC
14 October 2021